MY SIDEWALKS ON
SCOT
READING STREET

Adapting

Program Authors

Connie Juel, Ph.D.

Jeanne R. Paratore, Ed.D.

Deborah Simmons, Ph.D.

Sharon Vaughn, Ph.D.

ISBN: 0-328-21549-X
Copyright © 2008 Pearson Education, Inc.

Editorial Offices: Glenview, Illinois • Parsippany, New Jersey • New York, New York
Sales Offices: Boston, Massachusetts • Duluth, Georgia • Glenview, Illinois
Coppell, Texas • Sacramento, California • Mesa, Arizona

Adapting

Around Town 5

How do people adapt to changing communities?

Triumphs 31

How do we overcome physical challenges?

Around Town

Contents

Around Town

Words 2 the Wise

As cities grow, they must be changed to meet the people's needs. As you read, think about how your community has changed and how **people adapt** to these changes.

New Cities

People who plan cities always look for new designs that let people enjoy cities in safe ways.

In many cities builders design "green" buildings. These buildings save energy and water. They cut down on waste. And they use recycled materials. The buildings are called "green" because they protect the environment.

Let's see other ways cities are changing to protect the environment.

Solar panels collect the sun's energy during the day. The energy can be stored and used later.

Cleveland, Ohio, plans to spend as much as $2,200,000 to build a walkway and bike lane for this highway!

Biking

Cars pollute. Bikes don't! Some cities are working to add bike lanes along highways.

In Chicago, Illinois, the fountain in Millennium Park is a great place to splash around.

Green Space

Some cities are adding parks. The parks may include plants, flowers, structures, and sculptures.

Citizens put their recyclable waste in a bin that a recycling company later picks up.

Recycling

Cities are also recycling aluminum, glass, plastic, paper, and yard waste.

Many government and private buildings plant roof gardens to improve the environment.

Roof Gardens

Many people plant gardens on their roofs. Plants take in carbon dioxide. They give out oxygen. This process cleans the air.

OLD BUILDINGS, NEW USES

by John Stephenson

Union Station in St. Louis, Missouri, was once the busiest railroad station in the United States. Today it is used as a hotel and shopping mall.

WHAT HAPPENS TO OLD BUILDINGS?

What is the oldest structure or building you know? Do you know a story about the structure? Some people tear down an old structure because they want to build something in its place. The building could be used again for another purpose. There are people who see that old buildings have potential. They have new ideas for these buildings. These people want to salvage them because they can reuse old buildings for different purposes.

LIBRARY BECOMES MUSIC CENTER

Urban areas have many old buildings. In Chicago, a library became a performing arts center. The Hild Library opened in 1931. When a new library was opened just down the street in 1984, the old building was vacant for several years. The Old Town School of Folk Music needed more space. The School took over the old building in 1994. They opened it as a performing arts center and school in 1998.

The Old Town School of Folk Music in Chicago uses this building that once was a library.

You can see art shows in old jail cells.

POLICE STATION BECOMES ART GALLERY

The Mad Art Gallery in St. Louis, Missouri, is where artists can display their work. In the 1930s, this urban building was a police station. An artist saw that the building had potential to be an art gallery. Today art is displayed in the old police car garage. The police sergeant's desk is sometimes used to serve snacks. The jail cells are now used for art shows. Now this police station is an urban space where people meet, talk, and have fun.

People who visit Brucemore Mansion enjoy seeing photographs that show how people lived in the mansion in the past.

MANSION BECOMES CULTURAL CENTER

The Brucemore Mansion was built in 1886 in Cedar Rapids, Iowa. Margaret Douglas Hall was the last person to own this rural, twenty-one-room mansion. She wanted her home to be a place where people could participate in cultural activities. So the mansion became a community cultural center after she passed away.

Today Brucemore Mansion is open to everyone. Visitors attend music concerts. People who love nature take walks in the garden. The mansion also has plays, musicals, and plant sales.

This building was the state capitol of Illinois from 1839 to 1876.

President Abraham Lincoln

STATE CAPITOL BECOMES MUSEUM

The Old State Capitol in Springfield, Illinois, was built in 1839. It was in this building that young Abraham Lincoln prepared court cases and speeches.

In 1966 this historic building was taken apart, brick by brick. An underground parking lot and a storage center were built. Then the building was put back together as it once looked. Today the Old State Capitol in Springfield, Illinois, is a museum.

RAILROAD DEPOT BECOMES ART CENTER

The Atchison, Topeka & Santa Fe (AT&SF) Railroad Depot was built in rural Littleton, Colorado, in 1888. In those days, most Americans traveled by train. Depots were places for meeting people and saying good-bye.

In 1967 the AT&SF Depot was closed. Later a group raised money to move and restore this historic depot. Today it is the Depot Art Center. Local artists use this building to show their work and teach art classes.

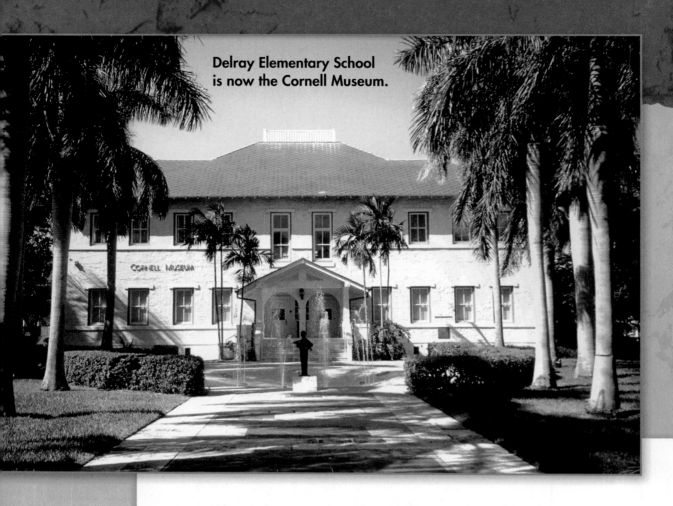

Delray Elementary School is now the Cornell Museum.

SCHOOL BECOMES MUSEUM

Sometimes old schools can be reused too. Delray High School in Florida was built in 1925. In the 1980s it was closed. Today it is the Crest Theater, a 323-seat theater and performing arts center. The classrooms are used for teaching classes.

Delray Elementary School was built in 1913. It was also abandoned in the 1980s. Today it is the Cornell Museum of Art and History. The museum displays art and teaches about the history of Florida.

People work together to restore and reuse old buildings.

THE FUTURE OF REUSING BUILDINGS

People are starting to understand the importance of old buildings. Sometimes reusing structures saves the time and money necessary to get the materials needed to build new buildings. Salvaging them can also save history. People can use the same structures their ancestors did. But the space might be used in a very different way.

WHAT DO YOU THINK?

Why is it important to reuse old buildings?

17

The MYSTERIOUS BOULDER

by Thais Larissa
illustrated by Elizabeth Callen

A boulder over twelve-feet high and shaped like an egg probably wouldn't attract much attention in a forest. But one morning, we woke up to find a huge boulder in our small, suburban neighborhood. Some people said they heard a loud rumbling in the middle of the night. That was just the beginning of a mystery.

My brother Jake and I saw the boulder as we were walking to school. You couldn't miss it. It was in the middle of town!

It was big and gray with blue marks running through it. People were walking around it, touching the cold, wet, cracked surface.

There was a large crowd surrounding the boulder. Cars stopped and caused congestion in the streets. Police came to direct traffic.

"Wow!" I said. "How did this get here?"

At school everyone was talking about the boulder. No one knew where it had come from. I couldn't wait to go back and get a better look!

19

That afternoon people were circling the boulder.

"It's some kind of joke," said Ann.

"It could be a meteor," I joked.

"Dakota Indian tribes have known about boulders that move on their own for years," Mr. Rivers told us. "The planet goes through periods of stillness, and then there is a great motion. They call it Taku-Skan-Skan. It means 'that which moves.'"

Just then, the mayor of Northfork appeared in front of the crowd.

"Fellow townspeople," Mayor Armstrong said in a loud voice. "I assure you that we will get this ugly rock off our town's property."

The adults in the crowd cheered.

"I will break this rock with a jackhammer and cart away the pieces myself if I have to," Mayor Armstrong declared. "This thing is causing congestion. It's wasting space."

I turned toward Jake. Mayor Armstrong was very serious.

That weekend, Jake and I visited the boulder. We brought colored chalk and drew pictures on it. Mrs. Franklin's gardening group was having their weekly meeting there. People were playing chess.

Our community never got together like this! Everyone just worked or went to school and stayed inside. The boulder was changing our community.

On Monday Mayor Armstrong appeared again.

"You'll be happy to hear that I hired a company to remove this thing from our town's property," he announced.

The crowd grumbled.

Mayor Armstrong looked at the crowd and said, "I'm doing the town a favor by removing it."

"This *thing* is a part of our community," Mr. Finch replied. "We enjoy the boulder."

The crowd cheered.

"I'm sorry," Mayor Armstrong replied. "This boulder will be gone the day after tomorrow."

That night there was a terrible storm. Lightning and heavy winds knocked out power lines.

The next morning, the boulder was gone! Everyone was shocked. The weatherman said that the winds from the storm had probably blown it away.

The people of Northfork gathered where the boulder had been. Mayor Armstrong hurried there too.

"I guess we'll have to go back to our old way of life," Mrs. Franklin said sadly.

The next week, the mayor called a town meeting. He saw how the boulder had changed our community. We would build a park where the boulder had been.

The crowd cheered.

"We'll call it Boulder Park!" the mayor exclaimed.

On the night of the grand opening of Boulder Park, a news reporter announced that a large boulder had mysteriously appeared in a suburban town in Texas.

Jake and I looked at each other. "Taku-Skan-Skan," we whispered.

BOULDER PARK

What Do You Think?

How did the people of Northfork learn to live with the boulder?

MY COMMUNITY

People live in different communities. Communities can be urban or rural. They can be on an island, near mountains, or in the desert. They might be near parks or forests.

Some communities have many people. These communities can be busy and noisy. Others are quiet with few people.

Communities are in many different places.

Think About It

You can plan your own community. Start by thinking about where you live. Then think about what you would change and what would be the same. Here are some things to consider.

- How will the streets be designed? How will people get around?
- How will the buildings look? What will they be made of?
- What will make the community unique? Parks? Statues?

Buildings are made differently in different communities.

KEY

 railroad

 house

 fire station

 police station

 train station

 walking path

 pond

Make a Plan

Plan two blocks of the downtown. First, draw a grid like the one below. Then place buildings, bridges, or other structures where you want them. Add symbols like the ones in the key. Use the ideas on the next page or your own ideas in your drawing.

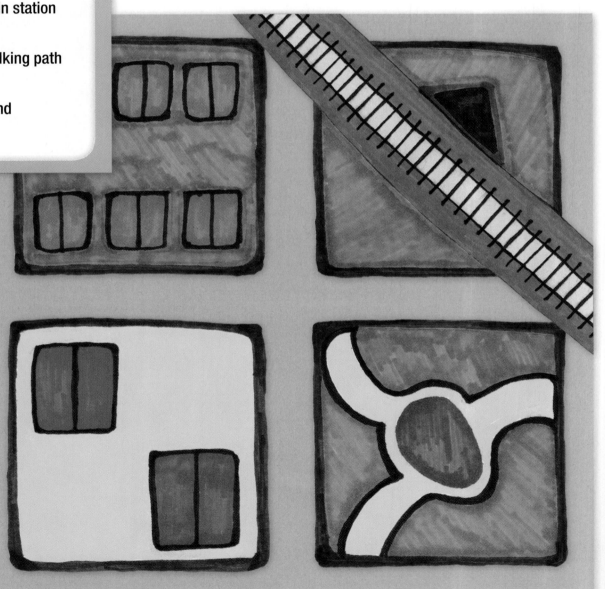

Places to Work and Shop

factory
bank
office
hospital
supermarket
restaurant
post office

Ways to Move Around

subway
bus
trolley
highway
sidewalk
bike path
street

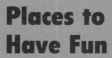

Places to Have Fun

park
sports arena
playground
movie theater
museum
library

Things to Make It Beautiful

statue
garden
flowers
fountain
pond
trees
park

Places to Live

house
apartment

4 You 2 Do

Word Play

Unscramble this week's concept vocabulary words.

rrlua   nabur

lasgeva   seeru

Making Connections

Think about a building in your neighborhood or town that isn't being used. Think of ways to put it to use.

On Paper

Your school has many rooms. Describe how one or two rooms might be used for a different purpose.

Triumphs

Contents

Triumphs

Let's Explore

Words 2 the Wise

We work to triumph over the challenges that we face. As you read, think about what it takes to **overcome physical challenges.**

33

BIONICS

Hands, arms, eyes, and ears are like tools. These tools can help people pick up a fork, listen to music, and write. What happens when these tools are damaged or do not work?

This mechanical hand works just like a human hand.

With the help of a bionic leg, this boy can ride a bike.

Scientists and inventors study how hands, ears, and other body parts work. They test ideas. They try new materials. Then they create devices* that give people back the tools they need.

*devices tools for a special purpose

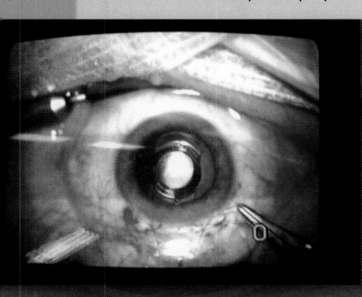
Tiny video cameras help doctors perform eye surgery.

This bionic hand was designed for a 2-year-old girl.

THREE WHO BEAT THE ODDS

by Lorraine McCombs

Sarah Reinertsen

When Sarah Reinertsen (RY-nert-sen) was born in 1975, her parents discovered a problem. Sarah's left leg was not healthy. When she was seven years old, her doctors and family made a decision. The doctors would amputate, or remove, her left leg. Sarah would have to adapt to using an artificial leg. An artificial body part is a prosthesis (pros-THEE-sis).

Sarah went through rehabilitation. She practiced exercises over and over again and learned to walk with her new leg.

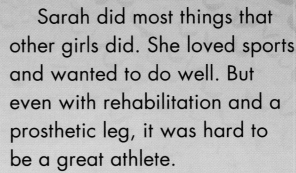

Sarah did most things that other girls did. She loved sports and wanted to do well. But even with rehabilitation and a prosthetic leg, it was hard to be a great athlete.

When Sarah was 11 years old, she went to her first track meet. She didn't feel so different there. She raced with other girls who used prosthetic legs. She won a race! After that first victory, Sarah couldn't be stopped.

In one competition, Sarah swam 2.4 miles, biked 112 miles, and ran 26.2 miles.

Sarah triumphs because of her skill and determination.

Sarah went on to compete in triathlons (try-ATH-lons). In a triathlon, the athletes run, then swim, and finally bike to the finish line. The athlete with the best time wins.

Sarah also was a member of a Paralympic (pair-uh-LIM-pik) Team. The top disabled athletes compete in these events. Sarah not only competed, but she also set world records.

Sarah followed her dream to be an athlete even with her physical disability. Her success inspires others to follow their dreams.

Emmanuel Ofosu Yeboah

A person with a disability needs good medical care. Emmanuel Ofosu Yeboah (oh-FOH-soo yeh-BOH-uh) had a weak right leg that made him unable to walk or work. He lives in Ghana (GAH-nuh), Africa. Medical help is hard to find for most people in Ghana.

Emmanuel didn't want to depend on others. He was determined to find a better life.

As a young child with a disability, Emmanuel did not have role models of others who overcame disabilities.

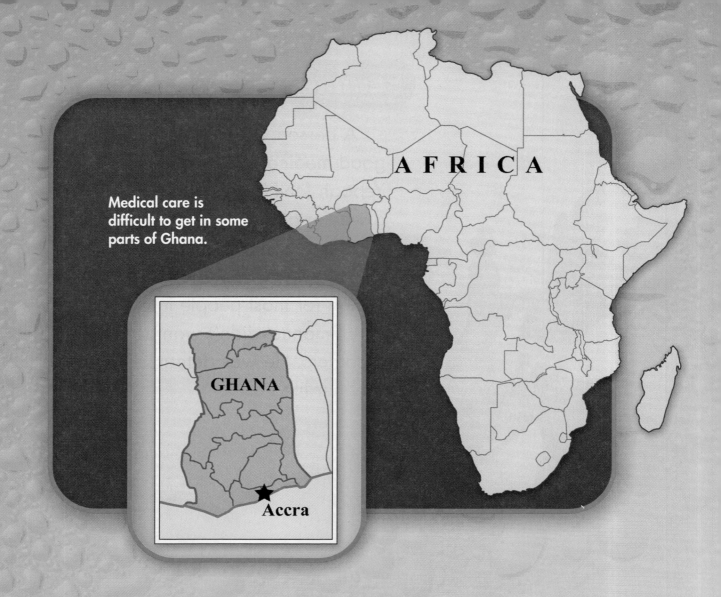

AFRICA

Medical care is difficult to get in some parts of Ghana.

GHANA

★ Accra

When Emmanuel was 13 years old, he started a shoeshine business. Emmanuel also wanted to ride a bike across Ghana. His plan was to show others he could be successful even with his disability.

He contacted the Challenged Athlete Foundation (CAF). This group gave Emmanuel a new bike and athletic clothing. Using only one leg, Emmanuel rode 380 miles across Ghana.

CAF continued to support Emmanuel. He flew to California and competed against other challenged athletes.

Emmanuel later received medical treatment and a new leg. For the first time he was able to stand up.

One success followed the other. He won a $25,000 award, but he decided to give most of it to help disabled people in Ghana. He gave the rest to CAF. Emmanuel proved that when you believe in yourself, nothing is impossible.

Other people with disabilities have successfully competed in bike races.

Bethany returned to surfing soon after losing her arm.

Bethany Hamilton

It was a warm day in Hawaii. A thirteen-year-old surfer paddled out into the ocean and waited for a wave. Suddenly, a shark appeared. It violently jerked the surfer, but she hung on to her surfboard. The shark swam away, but the girl had lost an arm.

This is the story of Bethany Hamilton, a talented surfer. After the attack, Bethany needed rehabilitation to relearn simple paddling movements.

Bethany's father was sure she would adapt. But Bethany's injury was a challenge for her doctors. It was difficult to make a prosthetic arm that fit at the shoulder. Finally, Bethany decided to be an athlete without using an artificial arm. In less than a month, she was on the water again.

Bethany planned to be in a triathlon, so CAF gave her a bike. Emmanuel rode a bike with one leg. Now Bethany planned to ride with one arm.

These are only three stories, but many athletes have overcome physical challenges. With the right attitude and the support of others, they became winners!

Bethany has the support of her family and fellow surfers. She also believes in herself.

What Do You Think?

How are these athletes different from each other? How are they the same?

43

Lee's New Goal

by Amie Jane Leavitt
illustrated by Jane McCreary

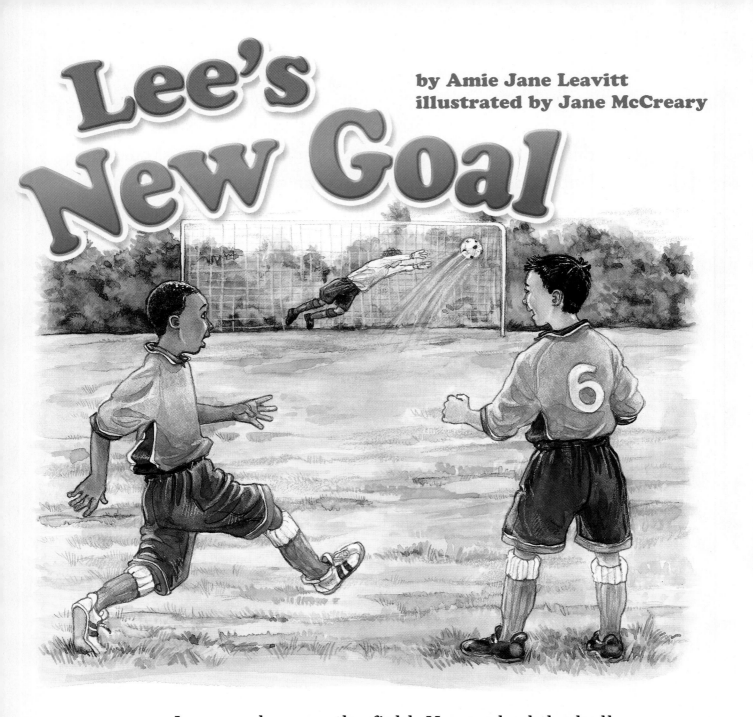

Lee raced across the field. He reached the ball and stopped it with his right foot. He passed it to Mike, who was flying down the side of the field. The pass was perfect! Mike didn't miss a stride. He shot confidently and scored. Goal!

"Nice pass, Lee," Mike said as they jogged together. The rest of the team shouted and whooped. They grinned as their friends cheered.

Lee was the star of the soccer team. He was the top passer, and he had the most goals on the team. He also was a good defender.

Lee just wished he could be as successful in the classroom as he was on the field.

Lee's new teacher, Ms. Myers, seemed nice. During the first week of class she announced an important assignment. Each student would have to choose a book and write a three-page book report.

Book Report
3 pages

A whole book! That wasn't a big deal for most of the kids, but it would be a great challenge for Lee. He had a learning disability called dyslexia. He had trouble reading.

Mike asked him once to describe what it was like.

"Sometimes I stare at the words but the letters are mixed-up. The words don't make sense," Lee had replied. "I can't remember the sounds the letters are supposed to make. I'm fast with a soccer ball, but I feel slow with a book."

"Now I know why you never volunteer to read," said Mike.

When he had to read aloud in school, he would panic. Butterflies seemed to flutter around inside his stomach.

Lee went to talk with Ms. Myers. "I'm worried about the book report because of my dyslexia," he said.

"I don't want you to be worried, Lee," Ms. Myers said. "I'll work with you."

"First, I'd like you to talk with another teacher, Mr. Miller," she continued. "He knows a lot about dyslexia."

Lee met Mr. Miller after school. He was very friendly.

"I have dyslexia, and I've tried to learn to read better, but I can't seem to make much progress," Lee explained.

"I know how you feel," Mr. Miller said. "I have dyslexia too."

Wow! Lee thought. *A successful adult who has dyslexia.* He felt relieved and full of hope. "How did you get to be a teacher?"

Mr. Miller smiled. "If you persist, you can improve your reading. A lot of people have dyslexia, including famous artists and scientists. Thomas Edison probably had it. He was a very poor student as a boy. But he ended up making over a thousand inventions."

"So, what do you do?" Lee asked. "How can I fix this?"

"There isn't any quick fix," Mr. Miller said, "but persistence pays off. Keep working with your reading teacher. Listen to her suggestions. I'll help you too."

Lee explained that he had to read a book and write a report.

"Good. We have a goal," Mr. Miller replied. "Let's get started."

Lee and Mr. Miller started working on reading after school. At first Lee could not see any difference, but slowly his reading improved.

Now it was time to choose a book to read. Lee found a biography of the artist and inventor Leonardo da Vinci (lee-uh-NAR-doh duh-VIN-chee). Lee learned that Leonardo might have had dyslexia.

Lee rushed home every day, looking forward to reading his book. Some days it was a struggle, but he was determined to persist. After several weeks, Lee was reading more confidently.

When Lee got an A on his book report, he ran to see Mr. Miller.

"Nice going, Lee," Mr. Miller said with a smile.

It was like a cheer. And Lee felt as if he had just kicked a winning goal!

What Do You Think?

How were Lee's feelings about the project different before he worked with Mr. Miller and after?

Shooting for the Stars

See how overcoming challenges brought these people success!

Wilma Rudolph

Don't blink. You might miss Wilma Rudolph! Wilma could not walk because of a disease called polio. By age 12, she had learned to walk again. In 1960 Wilma became the first American woman to win three gold medals in the Olympics.

Wilma Rudolph did not let anything stand in her way.

Franklin Delano Roosevelt

Polio didn't stop Franklin Delano Roosevelt from becoming President. The disease kept him from using his legs and feet so he used a wheelchair. He fought polio as he led Americans through the Great Depression and World War II.

FDR was the only President to be elected for more than two terms.

Turlough O'Carolan

Turlough O'Carolan (TER-loh oh-KAIR-oh-luhn) lost his sight because of smallpox. But he didn't let that stop him. He took a horse and his harp and traveled with a guide. He entertained audiences throughout Ireland and composed over 220 tunes.

Today Turlough O'Carolan's harp is on display at the National Museum of Ireland.

Jackie Robinson was the first African American major league baseball player.

Jackie Robinson

Jackie Robinson earned a place in the Baseball Hall of Fame in 1962. Later he also battled diabetes. People with diabetes are often tired. They must check their blood sugar, eat right, and exercise. They can have healthy lives, just like Jackie Robinson!

George Washington

Did you know that George Washington had trouble reading? Some experts believe he had dyslexia. With this disability, words and numbers look mixed-up and out of order. Washington became a great leader and our first President.

George Washington led the colonial army to victory over Britain during the Revolutionary War.

Albert Einstein

Albert Einstein was a famous scientist. Some people believe that he struggled with dyslexia. He faced challenges in reading and taking tests. Einstein won the Nobel Prize for physics in 1921.

In 1979, a memorial was built in Washington, D.C. to honor Albert Einstein.

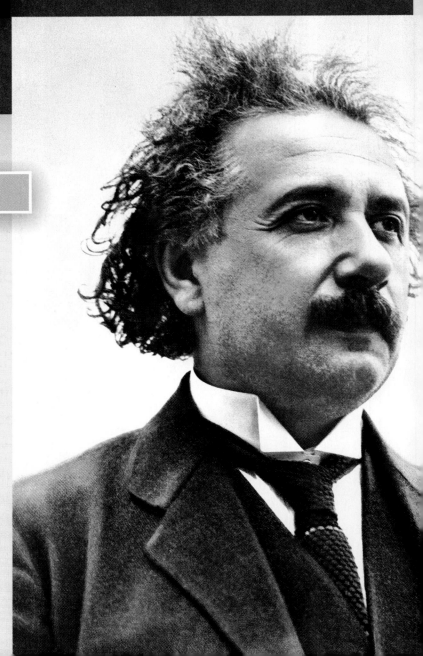

Ludwig van Beethoven

Ludwig van Beethoven was famous for his piano performances. He slowly lost his hearing. He was determined not to give up music, so he continued to compose. Beethoven wrote many symphonies* before completely losing his hearing.

*symphonies detailed music for orchestras

Beethoven wrote nine symphonies, the "Moonlight" Sonata, and other classical pieces.

Harriet Tubman

Harriet Tubman escaped from slavery in 1848. She led slaves to freedom. Harriet had a condition that causes people to fall into a deep sleep for a short time. Tubman didn't let her illness stop her work for freedom.

Every March 10, Harriet Tubman is honored for the work she did to help fight slavery.

4 YOU 2 DO

Word Play

Use the letters in the word **REHABILITATION** to create as many smaller words as you can.

Making Connections

Lee was afraid to read his book because of his dyslexia. What would Emmanuel, Sarah, or Bethany say to him about reaching a goal?

On Paper

Think about your senses: sight, smell, taste, hearing, touch. Which is the most important to you? Why?

Possible answers to Word Play: able, habit, relation, bite, inhabit, retail, hire, ration, air, rail, rate

Transformers

Contents

Transformers

Words 2 the Wise

Many animals have to **transform** to adapt to new environments. As you read, think about what you know about animal adaptation.

Can you find the walking stick in this picture?

Camouflage

What if your life depended on playing hide-and-seek? The walking stick is an insect named for its disguise. It can look for food without becoming someone else's lunch!

Some animals use their shapes or patterns to camouflage themselves. They even change their colors to match the seasons. For example, Arctic foxes are brown in summer and white in winter.

The coat of an Arctic fox turns white in the winter.

60

Certain animals blend into the trees, bushes, and plants around them. They hide from a predator* this way.

In Australia a bird called the tawny frogmouth looks like a dead branch when it is sleeping. The bird can rest safely without being bothered by its enemies.

Rabbits, bears, crabs, chameleons, and moths all use camouflage to hide.

*predator animal that feeds on other animals

This tawny frogmouth's colors help keep it safe from enemies.

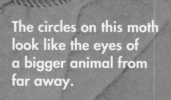

The circles on this moth look like the eyes of a bigger animal from far away.

Animals in the Wild!

by Alex Johnson

Once, all horses, pigs, cats, and dogs were wild. They didn't need people to take care of them. Then people began to tame these animals. They raised them for food, to work in fields, or as pets. The wild animals became domestic.

Sometimes domestic animals become wild again. When the Spanish came to North America, they brought domestic horses with them. Some of the horses got free. They are called feral horses.

These wild horses came from the horses that Spanish explorers brought to America.

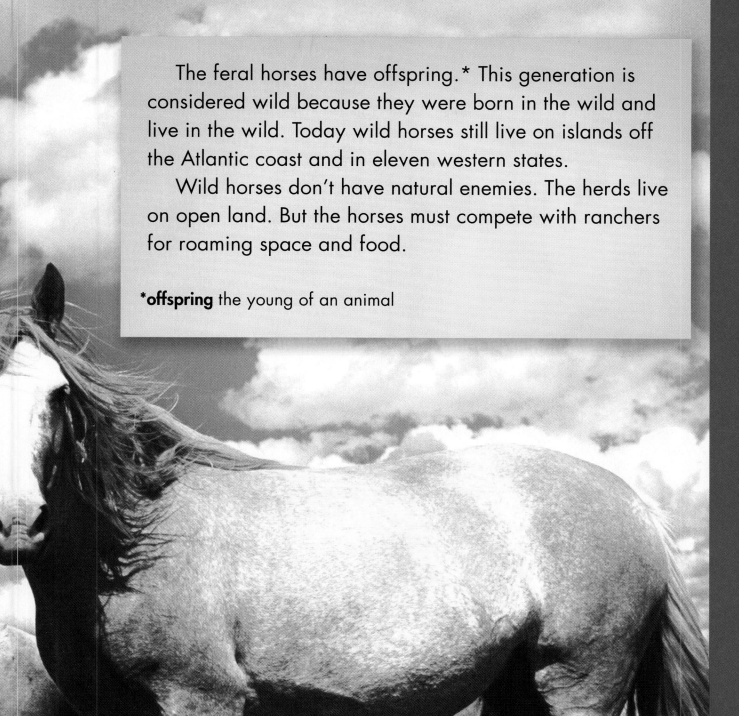

The feral horses have offspring.* This generation is considered wild because they were born in the wild and live in the wild. Today wild horses still live on islands off the Atlantic coast and in eleven western states.

Wild horses don't have natural enemies. The herds live on open land. But the horses must compete with ranchers for roaming space and food.

***offspring** the young of an animal

Domestic pigs are raised on farms.

Another animal that has gone wild is the hog. Feral hogs are related to the pigs that Spanish explorers brought to America.

Today's wild hogs are tougher than their ancestors. They are bigger too. They weigh from 100 to over 400 pounds! They can live in the woods or where only a few trees grow. More than two million feral hogs roam just in Texas.

Feral hogs roam freely.

Feral hogs will eat almost anything. They eat grass, seeds, snails, mushrooms, acorns, insects, and dead animals. They also love corn, rice, wheat, potatoes, and fruit. They are a big problem for some farmers.

Feral hogs come out mostly at night. The darkness is their camouflage. They transform the area. They roll on the ground. They leave big, bare patches in the grass.

This farmland has been damaged by feral hogs.

People began having cats and dogs as pets thousands of years ago. Over time, these animals became common household pets.

Some domestic cats and dogs get lost or are abandoned by their owners. These cats and dogs often "go wild," or become feral. They live anywhere they can find shelter. Many of them live in abandoned buildings or cars. They often eat garbage to survive. Their behaviors transform too.

Feral cats often hide from humans and only come out at night.

You should never try to pet a dog that is roaming free without an owner.

Feral cats are small and usually weigh only three to eight pounds. Over generations their fur color changes and blends in with the bushes in the country. It is their camouflage.

It's difficult to tell if a dog is feral or domestic. The main clue is how a dog behaves toward people. Feral dogs don't trust humans. It is difficult to adopt and tame these animals.

Feral cats and dogs can become a problem. They may be unfriendly toward neighborhood pets. They often carry diseases that can be spread to other animals and people.

People should stay away from all feral cats and dogs. It's safest to call an animal shelter if you want to help a feral animal.

Call your local animal shelter to find out how to help feral cats and dogs.

The best way to help is to prevent pets from becoming feral animals. Pet owners should never abandon a cat or dog. All pets need a collar with the owner's phone number on it. If a pet gets lost, someone can bring it back to the owner.

All animals were originally wild creatures. Some animals have adapted to living with humans. These pets need humans to survive, but others, like horses and hogs, can return to the wild.

What Do You Think?

How does a domestic animal become feral?

Monk at Home

by Rachel Mann
illustrated by John Sandford

Devin shook flakes into Goldy's bowl. "You're cute, Goldy," he said. "But you're so boring. All you do is swim in circles." He turned to his mother. "Mom, I want a new pet."

"We don't have space in this little apartment," Mom explained.

"You can always visit the zoo," Dad suggested. "It's only two blocks away."

"But I want a pet that I can play with and nurture," Devin argued.

The next day, Devin and his parents were watching the evening news.

"We just got word that a young spider monkey is missing from the zoo," the reporter said. "The zoo is asking anyone who has seen the monkey to call the zoo immediately."

"That's terrible," Dad said. "I hope they find the little guy, because he won't survive in the city."

A thought popped into Devin's mind. *A monkey would make a great pet!*

Devin went upstairs to do his homework. When he opened the door to his room, he heard papers rustling. The window was open.

It must be the wind Devin thought. Suddenly, a monkey jumped onto the desk!

"You must be the monkey from the zoo!" Devin said.

The monkey started jumping wildly.

"Awesome!" Devin said. "I have a pet monkey! I'll call you Monk."

"Dinner is ready," Dad called.

"Okay," Devin called back. "I'll try to sneak some food up for you," he whispered to Monk.

Devin went downstairs to eat dinner. He wondered what Monk liked to eat. Chicken? Broccoli? No, not for a monkey. He grabbed a banana and stuffed it into his pocket.

After dinner, Devin hurried back to his room. It was a disaster! Monk had ripped off the bed sheets, pulled the pictures off the wall, and thrown books off the shelves.

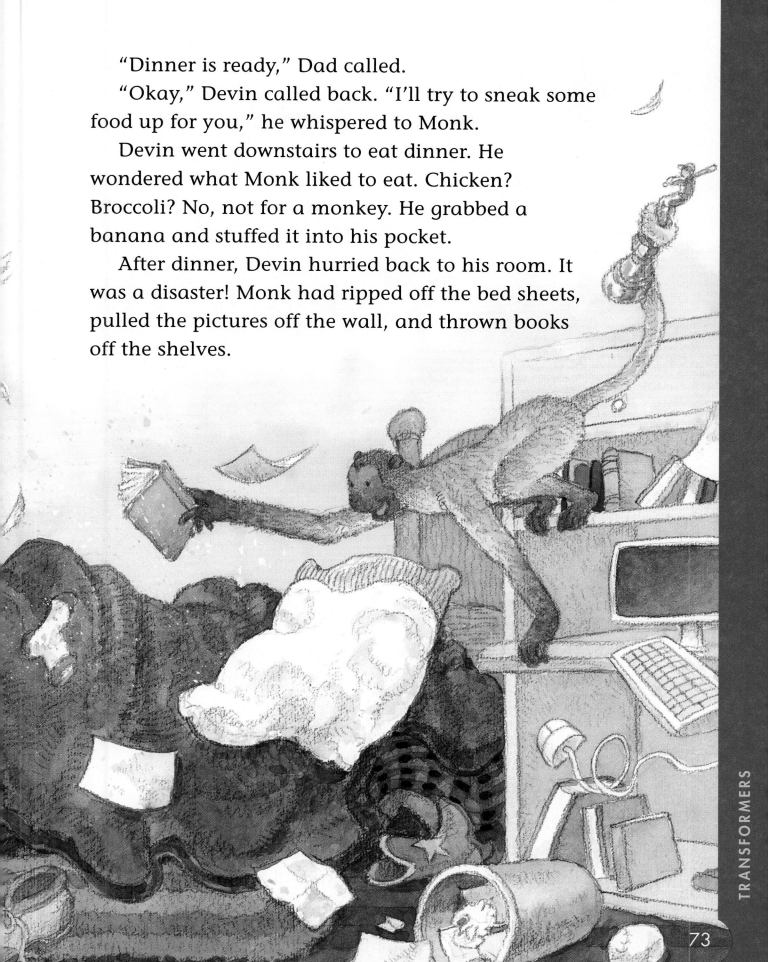

73

"What am I going to do? I don't know what a monkey needs!"

Devin put a blanket on the monkey. Then he searched on his computer for information about spider monkeys.

He learned that spider monkeys eat, play, and sleep in trees. They hardly ever come down to the ground. They eat fruits and seeds. They live together with their families, and young monkeys stay close to their mothers.

Monk stared out the window. Did Monk miss his mother?

Devin thought about what the reporter had said earlier. "I want to adopt you as my pet," he said to Monk. "But I just can't nurture you the way your family can. I know what I have to do."

Devin went downstairs. "Mom, Dad," he said. "I have something I need to tell you."

"What is it?" asked Mom.

"I know where the monkey from the zoo is," he said. "It's in my room."

"What?" Mom and Dad gasped.

Devin explained how Monk had climbed through his open window.

The family decided to call the zoo. Carol, a zoo worker, said she would be right over.

When Carol arrived, she put Monk into a cage.

"You did the right thing by calling us," she told Devin. "Would you like to come to the zoo? You can be there when we reunite this monkey with its mother."

At the zoo Devin and his parents watched as Monk swung into his mother's arms.

The next night at dinner, Devin wasn't hungry.

Mom asked, "Did you visit Monk at the zoo today?"

Devin shrugged. "I went. It wasn't the same."

Mom and Dad exchanged looks. "Devin, go into the kitchen and get more milk," Mom said.

When Devin opened the door he shouted, "Wow!"

A puppy came running toward him.

"I think I'll name him Monk Junior!" Devin said.

What Do You Think?

What steps did Devin take to nurture the monkey?

The Anglerfish

by Douglas Florian

Lurking on the ocean floor
There works a crafty carnivore.
The anglerfish has set a trap
With its dangling, fleshy flap,
Complete with fishing pole and bait,
And all it has to do is wait
For some poor fish to take the lure
And make the ocean one fish fewer.

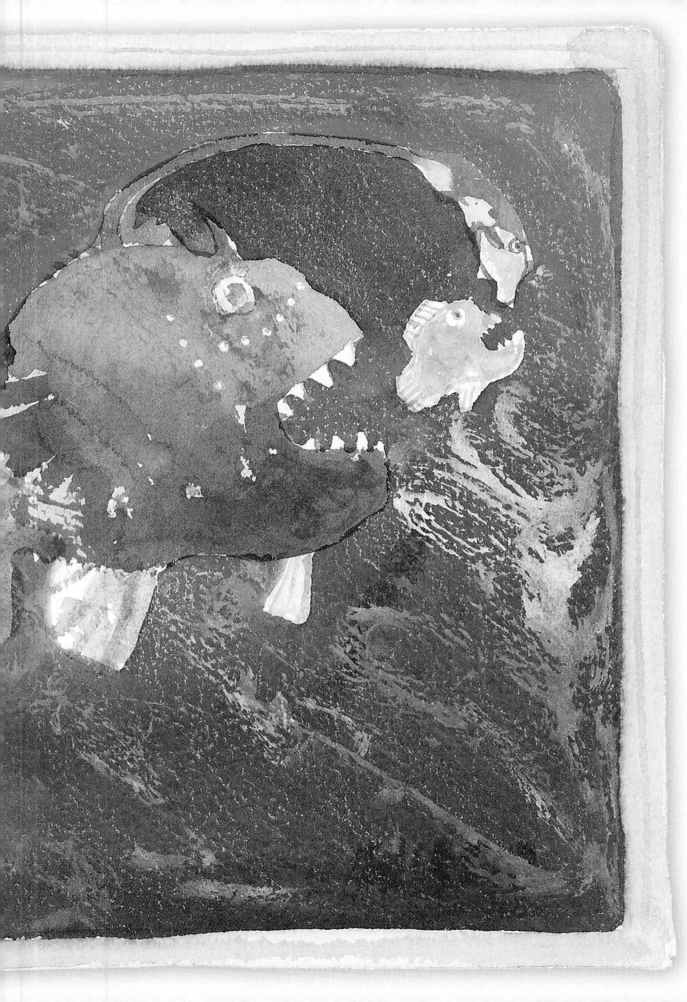

The Ray

by Douglas Florian

Grand and gray
The regal ray
Slyly g l i d e s
Upon its prey.
It almost flies
On weightless wings.
Its whiplike tail
With poison stings.
All creatures near
This royal ray
Retreat in fear:
Make way!
Make way!

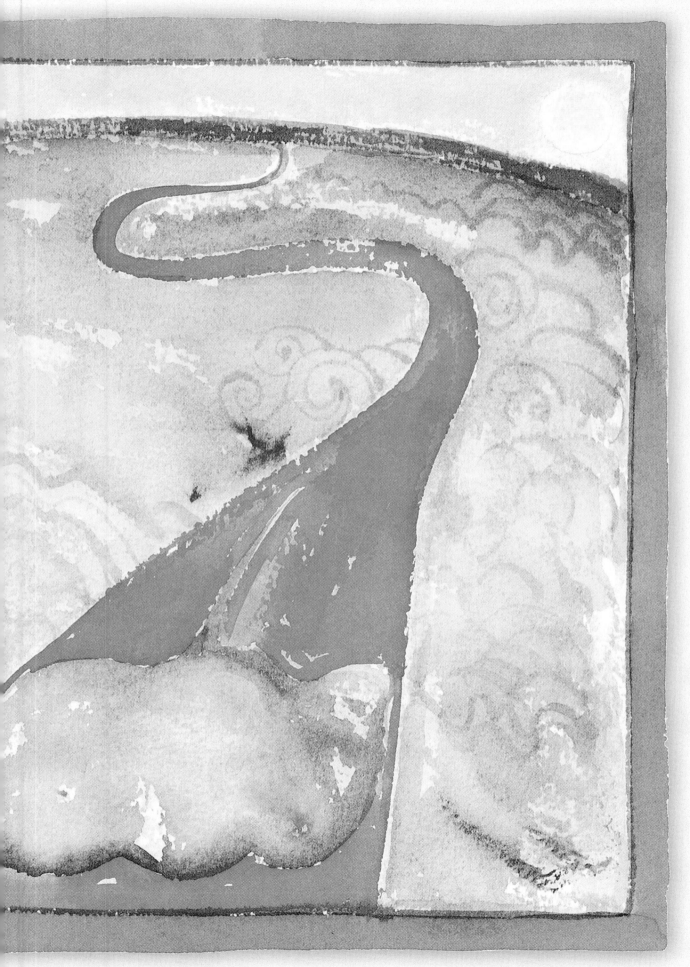

4 you 2 Do

Word Play

Unscramble these words:

flera

toscdeim

osfmratnr

Now see how many animal names you can make using these letters. You may use each letter more than once and mix letters from different words.

Making Connections

Do you think wild animals could be pets? Explain why or why not.

On Paper

Which wild animal would you like to have as a pet? Why?

Answers to Word Play: feral, domestic, transform

New Places

Contents

New Places

Words 2 the Wise

People must adapt to new places. As you read, think about how you have had to **adapt to new places** or situations.

Where We Live

People from different places wear different kinds of clothes. They live in different kinds of houses and eat different foods.

In hot climates, people wear light clothing. It protects them from the sun. In cold climates, they dress in more than two layers of clothing to trap their bodies' warmth.

This boy's traditional clothing protects him from the sun and heat.

86

Around the world, homes are built to work in the environment. Large cities are often crowded. Every bit of land is used. So builders build skyscrapers. In forest regions, houses might be built of wood. In dry, hot places, there isn't much wood. Homes are often made of brick or stone. In marshy* areas, a home might be built on long wood poles called stilts.

***marshy** like a marsh; wet, soft land

Houses in the northeast United States are built with steep roofs because that area gets a lot of snow. This way, the snow slides off the roof instead of weighing it down.

Clothes are not just for protection and comfort. They can also show who you are and where you are from.

Tall buildings line city streets.

Fish and seafood are popular dishes in places near the sea. Oranges, lemons, and other citrus fruits are easy to find in warm climates. Wheat and corn need flat open fields and lots of warm weather to grow. Cattle* need open grazing land. One place this is found is the western United States.

*cattle animals, such as cows, raised for meat, milk, or hides

Houses are built differently in different climates.

People have learned to adjust to their environments. Houses, clothing, and food tell about environment. Scientists studying 5,000 year old trash piles found that when climates changed, people's habits changed too.

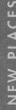

Sticks and

Apartment buildings are common in towns and cities. But many styles of homes are found in only one region of the world. Let's visit buildings around the world to learn why they look as they do.

In the city of Caracas (kuh-RAH-kus), Venezuela, a famous architect named Carlos Villanueva (VEE-ya-noo-AY-vuh) designed many buildings.

New York

Tokyo

Buildings in one city may look similar to buildings in another part of the world.

Stones
by Usha Kent

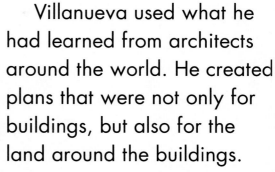

Villanueva used what he had learned from architects around the world. He created plans that were not only for buildings, but also for the land around the buildings.

Villanueva learned to modify how buildings in cities were built. He built apartments, colleges, and other buildings in Venezuela.

This building in Venezuela designed by Carlos Villanueva is 56 stories high.

The design of these houses is thousands of years old.

The land around Syria (SEER-ee-uh) has few trees for wood or other building materials. These beehive-shaped houses are built of straw and mud brick. They stay cool during the day and warm at night. The shape of the roof makes it stand up well to strong winds and even earthquakes.

Beehive houses are rare now. More and more people build with concrete. Lifestyles change. People want more comforts. The builder must modify the design to fit the lifestyle.

In Wales in the United Kingdom another old building design is the stone castle. Some of these castle walls are five feet thick. They are made of solid rock. It can get cold in Wales, but that is not why builders made the thick walls. These castles were fortresses. They were meant to protect the people inside from enemy attacks. These castles are rare today.

This castle is one of the largest castles in Wales, Scotland, or England.

Farmhouses and cottages in Wales are also built of stone. They have big fireplaces to warm rooms in the winter. Over time, people's lifestyles changed and they could turn a switch to get heat. A formal dining room for fancy dinner parties might become a game room or TV room.

There was a lot of stone available for building houses in Wales.

Hot air from this heater
would move through pipes
to heat the house.

Winters are cold in Korea. Long ago, Koreans heated
the space under the stone floor of their homes.

Hot air moved through pipes connected to a kitchen
heater that burned wood. People sat on the warm floor
to eat. They also slept on mats on the warm floors.

Today Korean homes are heated by pipes that carry hot
water under the floors. People in many countries, including
the United States, are beginning to use this kind of heat.

Houses are often made from materials that can be found easily. That is why Inuit (IN-yoo-it) people of the Arctic regions made houses of snow called igloos.

An igloo has a rounded shape. The blocks are pressed together. Igloos can withstand hurricane-force winds. Inuit people live in igloos during the hunting season. They return to their homes when it is over.

Inuit people build a traditional igloo.

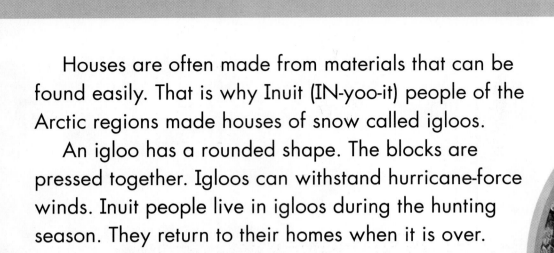

People use recycled materials to build houses.

A very unusual building material is garbage! Some people make homes using old tires. They shred the tires and mix them into a cement solution. Others use cans or glass bottles.

The environment affects how we dress, what we eat, and where we live. How does it affect you?

What Do You Think?

How do people choose materials for buildings?

SCHOOLS
Then and Now

BY JOSHUA THOMPSON

A famous architect had a rule about buildings. He said that how a building would be used was most important. How the building looked came second.

Look at your classroom. Everything about the room is designed to help you learn. The same has been true of schools throughout history.

Schools have changed a lot over time. The needs of the people who use the schools have changed over time. School buildings have had to adjust to these changing needs.

Today's schools meet today's needs.

ONE ROOM FOR ALL GRADES

Try to imagine what school was like in 1900. In some farming areas, schoolhouses had one room, one or two windows, and a fireplace. Benches for the students lined the walls. All of the students learned in one classroom. There was one teacher for all grades. Five-year-old children were taught in the same room as 14-year-olds.

In 1900, some schools had just one room.

But there weren't a lot of students in farming areas. One building was enough for all of the children from nearby families. A house was big enough—a schoolhouse!

In farm communities, children were often needed on the farm. Teachers were accustomed to adjusting their lessons because students might not be present every day.

In farm towns, not all students were in school every day.

SCHOOLS CHANGE WITH COMMUNITIES

As communities grew, school buildings evolved. Benches on the walls became rows of tables or desks for students. They used pens that needed to be refilled with ink many times. The desks had holes for inkwells. Later, desks of different sizes for students of different ages were added.

Later schoolhouses might have additional rooms, even though all the teaching still took place in one room.

Students of all ages would be taught in the same classroom.

Many early schoolhouses had a tower with a bell, which the teacher or a student rang by pulling a rope. The schoolhouse was not just for the students. The schoolhouse was an important building for meetings and other events. The bell could alert the community to help in an emergency or that a meeting was starting.

The bell with a rope became an electric bell as electricity reached farming areas. Now what do you hear when recess ends? It might be music or a buzzer.

Bell towers on early schoolhouses called students to class.

As towns grew in farming areas, there were even more students. By the 1920s, it was clear that one-room schoolhouses wouldn't work.

More teachers were needed, and different classrooms were needed for different grades. One way schools evolved was to separate students by their ages. What ages are the students in your school? Is there a high school in your school building?

As farming towns grew larger, the schoolhouses grew too.

FROM CHALKBOARDS TO VIDEO SCREENS

The tools in the classrooms changed too. In the past, desks were bolted to the floor in rows. Students might also be seated side by side at long tables.

Later students had separate desks. They had a top with a hinge, so students could keep their pencils and books inside the desk.

Now most desks can be moved around. There might be a shelf under the desk for books. Many students learn at round tables.

The ways classrooms are arranged have changed to meet the needs of today's classes.

Look at your classroom. Is there a whiteboard or chalkboard? In 1900 the teacher would have written on a black slate with white chalk. Now many teachers are accustomed to presenting lessons on the classroom video screen.

So much has changed about schools. Today's classrooms seem to have little in common with the classrooms of 1900. But the goal of school hasn't changed. Students are still taught what they need to know to succeed in the world!

Computers play an important role in today's classroom.

What Do You Think?

How have schools changed over time?

My House

If you could live anywhere in the world, where would it be? What would your house look like? Here's your chance to design your own house.

1 First, decide where you want to live. Is it hot or cold? Wet or dry? Is it high up on a mountain, on the beach, or in a river valley? How much rainfall does this place get, and how often?

2 Now think about the shape of your house. Does it have a peaked roof or a flat one? Does it have flat walls with corners or smooth, curved walls?

3 What will you use to build your house? How will you change the design to match the climate where you want to live?

4 How big will it be? How many rooms? Are they all on one floor? Is part of your house underground?

5 Draw a picture of your house.

6 Draw a floor plan of your house.

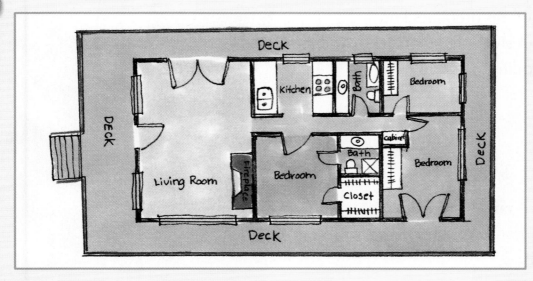

7 Share your new house with friends!

4 You 2 Do

Word Play

Be an architect of words! What other words can you build from the word below?

ARCHITECT

Making Connections

Architects learn about climates to help them design buildings. What should an architect know about students when designing a school?

On Paper

What might a school or a house of the future be like?

Possible answers for Word Play: arch, teach, chair, hit, race, hire, their, catch

Brand New Me

Contents

Brand New Me

Words 2 the Wise

There are many ways for us to improve ourselves. When you take care of your body, you feel brand new. As you read, think about the different ways you can **improve yourself.**

Healthy Living

Imagine a grocery cart filled with all the colors of the rainbow. If your meals have many bright colors, you are eating in a healthy way. Red apples, green lettuce on your sandwich, black bean soup, bright orange carrots, and cheeses make a colorful plate.

Don't forget to drink a glass of milk. Kids nine years or older should have three cups of milk each day. Do you like yogurt? You can eat it in place of milk.

Foods that are brightly colored aren't just eye-catching. They are packed with the most vitamins.

A diet full of fruits and vegetables helps give you all the right vitamins. Some nutrition studies show that children do not get enough calcium, potassium, fiber, or vitamin E. How can you get more? Choose from foods shown on this page.

Fiber

Whole wheat bread, oatmeal, and other grain cereals

Vitamin E

Sunflower seeds, almonds, and peanuts

Calcium

Yogurt, milk, and cheese

Potassium

Bananas, oranges, and spinach

Jump, Kick, Swim, Dance

Your body was meant to move. Walk the dog. Play basketball. Dance to your favorite music. Start a game of tag or find a jump rope partner. If you stay active and exercise, you will feel better.

Treat yourself after exercise. Eat an orange, an apple, or a banana. Drink a glass of fruit juice. You'll feel great!

Exercise is an important part of healthy living.

I like eating...

Think of five foods you enjoy eating. Which are natural foods? Which are processed foods? Did you think of popcorn or peanuts? Did you think of fruit juices? Did you think of fresh strawberries or pineapple? What about grilled chicken? These foods are good for you. They tempt your taste buds too. Many delicious foods are nutritious!

Combine different foods to get the right balance in your diet.

THE SECRETS OF KARATE

BY JEFF O'KELLEY

Have you ever watched a martial arts movie? Do you like to see Jackie Chan or Bruce Lee in action? If so, you would probably like karate!

Karate began as a way for people to learn how to protect themselves from an attack. Karate focused on self-defense. Students learned the weak spots of the human body. Today students practice karate as a form of exercise and use its teachings to learn discipline.

People can learn karate by taking classes or joining karate clubs.

Karate was called "the way of the open hand" because students fought without weapons.

Sea of Japan

JAPAN Tokyo

Pacific Ocean

Okinawa

WHERE DID KARATE COME FROM?

Karate is popular now, but it used to be kept secret. Some believe that karate is over a thousand years old.

Karate probably began in Okinawa (oh-kee-NAH-wah), Japan. It was used for protection. In the past it was against the law for some people in Okinawa to use weapons. They learned to protect themselves by using their hands. Karate developed over many years.

It takes great skill in karate to break a board.

Later, this form of fighting became illegal too. But the people had a strong motivation to learn karate. They studied it secretly.

Karate students kept no records of the movements they learned. The secrets of karate were not even shared among family members. But this martial art was passed on.

Over time karate spread to other countries, and each group added new movements. Karate changed, but its principles remained the same. Students only fought in self-defense.

KARATE TODAY

Karate eventually spread all over the world. The movements were not a secret any longer. People everywhere began to practice karate to stay healthy and learn discipline of the mind.

Karate is now a major sport. Karate movies are very popular as well. In the 1980s Americans watched *The Karate Kid* movies and found out how karate students learn discipline and skill. Recent movies, like *Crouching Tiger, Hidden Dragon,* made karate moves look like dancing.

Karate is an important part of the movie *Crouching Tiger, Hidden Dragon.*

WHAT DOES KARATE TEACH?

Students still learn self-defense as they study karate. But now most students practice karate to exercise and learn discipline. Karate helps students understand both their bodies and their minds. They must breathe correctly, think clearly, and react quickly.

Students also learn to respect others, and must always obey their *sensei* (SEN-say), or teacher. Students must repeat moves. Over time the moves become automatic. The motivation to do well must come from inside.

Karate students move arms, wrists, elbows, and shoulders carefully.

Karate belts come in many different colors.

BELTS CAN SAY A LOT

How can you tell how skilled karate students are? Look at the color of their belts. Beginners have white belts. Experts have black belts.

Some karate schools have yellow, brown, green, blue, white and black belts. Each belt shows a different rank.

Historians disagree over how the belts started. Some say fighters dyed their white belts as they got better. The belts eventually turned dark. The dark color became the sign of an expert.

Young karate students are encouraged by the system of belts. A new color is like graduating.

Students of karate learn skills that are thousands of years old while having fun!

Others believe that karate masters never washed their belts. The belts got so dirty from fighting that they turned black.

DO YOU HAVE WHAT IT TAKES?

You can learn karate too! It's great exercise. But more importantly, you'll learn the same principles that began in Okinawa! The sensei will teach you karate moves. The sensei will also teach the importance of peace. Karate is a way to defend oneself, exercise, and learn discipline!

As you study karate, you'll understand your own mind and body better. Students of karate learn discipline. They continue the traditions created long ago in Okinawa.

WHAT DO YOU THINK?

Why is discipline important in karate?

Champions!

by Uma Krishnaswami
illustrated by Joy Allen

Justine and Erica stepped up to the stage. Erica began telling the story that they hoped would win them tickets to the Live Boys concert.

"There *is* such a thing as having too much junk food in your diet. We learned this the hard way. A pie-eating contest actually taught us about nutrition!"

"Yes," Justine agreed. "It all started two weeks ago when we were skating by Pie Pals restaurant. Here's what happened . . ."

124

Justine stopped and pointed to the window. "Look! They're having a pie-eating contest next week! The winner gets tickets to the Live Boys concert."

Erica did not need any more motivation. The Live Boys was her favorite band. "We'll have to start training if we want to win."

Justine was skeptical. "What do you mean *we?* And what do you mean by *training?* How can you train for a pie-eating contest?"

125

"Please," Erica begged. "You have to enter the contest. Then we'll have two chances to win." She explained how they could get their bodies used to foods with more fat and sugar.

Justine shrugged. "I guess it wouldn't hurt us if we changed our diet...at least for a little while."

The girls agreed to start their new diet the next day. Only four things stood in their way—their parents.

That night Erica told her mom and dad about the contest. "I eat balanced meals. I like grains and lean meat. Fruits and vegetables are good too. But I need to eat more foods like cake and cookies. Then I can win."

"I can't agree with your plan," said Mom.

Dad shook his head. "Healthy eating shouldn't be experimental."

"People who don't eat healthy foods can have medical problems." Mom scooped chicken with vegetables onto Erica's plate.

"They gain weight, and they can damage their hearts," said Dad.

Erica ate the last forkful of carrots. "I thought junk food just causes cavities. That's why I wasn't supposed to eat it."

"That's true too," agreed Mom.

Dad asked, "How long do you think it will take until a poor diet makes you feel unhealthy?"

"Forever," Erica insisted. "I can eat foods with lots of sugar and fat. I will feel fine."

Mom and Dad looked at Erica. Erica looked back at them then sighed.

"Okay! Okay! I knew that eating junk food was not good for me. But I had no idea it could cause that many bad things to happen!" Her mom and dad smiled.

"Entering that pie-eating contest or training for it is just not worth it," said Erica, disappointed.

"We figured you'd make the right choice once you knew the facts!" said her dad confidently.

Erica saw Justine before class the next day. "Your parents called my parents last night and told them about our plan," said Justine.

"Did you get the lecture on nutrition that I got?" asked Erica. Justine nodded her head.

"Well, I guess that means no Live Boys for us," Justine replied.

"Don't count us out yet," Erica said as she pointed to a sign hanging in the library window.

Justine looked at the sign and then at Erica.

"Erica! The writing contest is about nutrition!" exclaimed Justine.

"Is there anything we *don't* know about it after last night?!" replied Erica.

All week long Erica and Justine brainstormed and organized their ideas. Then they wrote their essay. They were the last to turn it in on Friday. The next week, the principal announced them as winners.

"And that is how we became experts on balanced nutrition!"

What Do You Think?

How did the pie-eating contest help Justine and Erica?

What ARE You Eating?

Did you know that some of your favorite foods are the worst things for you? When was the last time you bit into a big, juicy burger? Was it overflowing with cheese and topped with greasy bacon? That one burger has more fat than you should eat in an entire day! Take a bite out of this!

> If you eat 60% of a burger—that's about 4 or 5 bites—you've already eaten all the fat you should for one day!

It's All on the Label!

Foods have nutrition labels that tell you exactly what you are eating. Many restaurants will tell you what's in their food too. Just ask!

This burger supplies your body with 71% of the calories that you need to eat today. You only have 29% left!

You've gone way over your limit! Your burger can fill 22 teaspoons with its 107 grams of fat!

Saturated fat is bad fat. One burger has more than twice the amount you should have in one day!

Your burger has enough sodium to fill more than one teaspoon with salt!

This burger doesn't give your body the fiber it needs. You still have to eat 1 1/2 cups of lima beans!

Your body needs protein to stay strong. But this burger gives you twice as much as you need for one day!

Nutrition Facts

Serving Size 1 Burger
Servings Per Container 1

Amount Per Serving

% Daily Value

Calories	1,410	71%
Total Fat	107g	165%
Saturated Fat	45g	225%
Cholesterol	229 mg	76%
Sodium	2,740mg	114%
Total Carbohydrate	47g	15%
Dietary Fiber	2g	8%
Sugars	9g	
Protein	60g	120%

Kids over four should eat about 2,000 calories every day. Look at the chart below. Let it guide you in your food choices.

Total Fat	Eat Less Than	65g
Saturated Fat	Eat Less Than	20g
Cholesterol	Eat Less Than	300mg
Sodium	Eat Less Than	2,400mg
Total Carbohydrates	Eat	300g
Dietary Fiber	Eat	25g

4 YOU 2 DO

Word Play

Pretend you own a restaurant that serves healthy foods. Use the words below on a sign to make people want to eat there.

diet

nutrition

balanced

Making Connections

How do discipline and a balanced diet help us improve ourselves?

On Paper

What type of exercise do you enjoy? What is your favorite healthy food?

Glossary

ac·cus·tomed (ə kus′ təmd), *ADJECTIVE*. used to; in the habit of: *I am accustomed to getting up early for school.*

a·dapt (ə dapt′), *VERB*. to change yourself; get used to something: *Animals have different ways to adapt to their environments.* **a·dapt·ed, a·dapt·ing.**

ad·just (ə just′), *VERB*.

1 to arrange; change to make fit: *He adjusted his glasses in order to see better.*

2 to get used to; become accustomed to: *Some wild animals never adjust to life in the zoo.*

a in hat	ō in open	sh in she
ā in age	ȯ in all	th in thin
â in care	ô in order	ŦH in then
ä in far	oi in oil	zh in measure
e in let	ou in out	ə =a in about
ē in equal	u in cup	ə =e in taken
ėr in term	ů in put	ə =i in pencil
i in it	ü in rule	ə =o in lemon
ī in ice	ch in child	ə =u in circus
o in hot	ng in long	

a·dopt (ə dopt′), VERB. to accept something as your own or as your own choice: *Ben will adopt a dog today at the animal shelter.*

ar·chi·tect (är′ kə tekt), NOUN. a person who designs and makes plans for buildings: *A famous architect designed the new skyscraper downtown.*

bal·anced (bal′ enst), ADJECTIVE. including an equal amount of different kinds of things: *Sam's balanced diet includes fruits and vegetables.*

cam·ou·flage (kam′ ə fläzh), NOUN. a disguised appearance that makes a person or animal look much like its surroundings: *The moth's camouflage protected it from its enemies.*

con·fi·dent·ly (kon′ fə dənt lē), ADVERB. with strong beliefs or certainty: *Susan confidently walked to the stage to give her speech.*

con·ges·tion (kən jes′ chən), NOUN. when an area is overcrowded: *The accident caused congestion on the highway.*

di·et (dī′ ət), NOUN. the group of foods and drinks that you can eat or drink: *My diet is made up of meat, fish, vegetables, grains, fruits, water, and milk.*

dis·ci·pline (dis′ ə plin), NOUN. training that helps someone learn to obey rules and control behavior: *The students show good discipline during fire drills.*

do·mes·tic (də mes′ tik), ADJECTIVE. not wild; tame: *Horses, dogs, cats, cows, and pigs are domestic animals.*

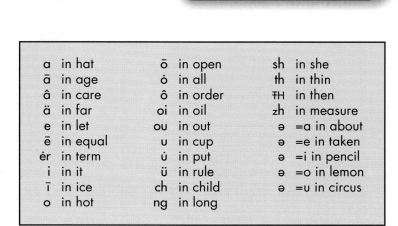

a in hat	ō in open	sh in she
ā in age	o˙ in all	th in thin
â in care	ô in order	ŦH in then
ä in far	oi in oil	zh in measure
e in let	ou in out	ə =a in about
ē in equal	u in cup	ə =e in taken
ėr in term	u˙ in put	ə =i in pencil
i in it	ü in rule	ə =o in lemon
ī in ice	ch in child	ə =u in circus
o in hot	ng in long	

dys·lex·i·a (dis lek′ sē ə), NOUN. difficulty in reading because the brain has difficulty recognizing different letters: *People with dyslexia sometimes see a word's letters in the wrong order.*

e·volve (i volv′), VERB. to change slowly over time: *School buildings have evolved to meet student's needs.* **e·volved, e·volv·ing.**

ex·er·cise (ek′ sər sīz), NOUN. an activity requiring physical effort to improve health: *Rollerblading is a good form of exercise.*

fer·al (fir′ əl), ADJECTIVE. gone back to the original wild condition after being tamed: *Cats can become feral animals after living on the streets.*

life·style (līf′ stīl′), NOUN. a person's or group's characteristic manner of living; style of life: *A healthy lifestyle includes eating properly and exercising.*

mod·i·fy (mod′ ə fī), VERB. to change something to make it better or different: *She learned to modify her schedule to include both sports and homework.* **mod·i·fied, mod·i·fy·ing.**

mo·ti·va·tion (mō′ tə vā′ shən), NOUN. something that makes you want to continue: *Getting a good report card was his motivation to study.*

nur·ture (nèr′ chər), VERB. to bring up; care for; train: *The mother dog nurtured her puppies until they could care for themselves.* **nur·tured, nur·tur·ing.**

nu·tri·tion (nü trish′ ən), NOUN. food; nourishment: *A balanced diet provides nutrition to keep our bodies strong.*

a in hat	ō in open	sh in she
ā in age	ȯ in all	th in thin
â in care	ô in order	ŦH in then
ä in far	oi in oil	zh in measure
e in let	ou in out	ə =a in about
ē in equal	u in cup	ə =e in taken
ėr in term	ù in put	ə =i in pencil
i in it	ü in rule	ə =o in lemon
ī in ice	ch in child	ə =u in circus
o in hot	ng in long	

per·sist (pər sist′), VERB.

1 to keep on doing something; refuse to stop: *She persisted in climbing the mountain even though it began raining.*

2 to last a long time: *On some very high mountains snow persists throughout the year.* **per·sist·ed, per·sist·ing.**

phys·i·cal (fiz′ ə kəl), ADJECTIVE. of or for the body: *She has great physical strength.*

po·ten·tial (pə ten′ shəl), NOUN. an ability or skill that may develop in the future: *She has potential to be a good basketball player if she practices.*

prin·ci·ple (prin′ sə pəl), NOUN.

1 a basic truth or law: *The principle of free speech is important in the United States.*

2 a rule or action or conduct: *One principle of karate is discipline.* PL. **prin·ci·ples.**

prop•er•ty (prop′ ər tē),
NOUN. something that
someone owns; possession
or possessions: *This house
is her property.*
PL. **prop•er•ties.**

rare (râr), *ADJECTIVE.* not happening often; unusual: *Snow is rare
in Florida.*

re•ha•bil•i•ta•tion (rē′ hə bil′ ə tā′ shən), NOUN. getting
something back to normal: *She was in rehabilitation for
her broken leg.*

re•use (rē yüz), *VERB.* to use again: *We will reuse the tablecloth
after we wash it.* **re•used, re•us•ing.**

a in hat	ō in open	sh in she
ā in age	ȯ in all	th in thin
â in care	ô in order	ᴛH in then
ä in far	oi in oil	zh in measure
e in let	ou in out	ə =a in about
ē in equal	u in cup	ə =e in taken
ėr in term	u̇ in put	ə =i in pencil
i in it	ü in rule	ə =o in lemon
ī in ice	ch in child	ə =u in circus
o in hot	ng in long	

rur·al (rŭr′ əl), *ADJECTIVE*. in the country; belonging to the country: *My grandparents live in a quiet, rural area an hour from the city.*

sal·vage (sal′ vij), *VERB.* to save property or goods after a fire, flood, or some other disaster: *After the fire, we were able to salvage some of the things in our house.* **sal·vaged, sal·vag·ing.**

sub·ur·ban (sə bėr′ bən), *ADJECTIVE.* just outside or near a city: *Many people who work in the city live in suburban areas.*

suc·cess·ful (sək ses′ fəl), *ADJECTIVE.* having the result that you hoped and planned for: *The class picnic was very successful.*

tame (tām), *VERB.* to take from the wild and make obedient: *The lion was tamed for the circus.* **tamed, tam·ing.**

trans·form (tran sfôrm′), *VERB.* to change the form or appearance of something: *The blizzard transformed the trees into mounds of white.* **trans·formed, trans·form·ing.**

ur·ban (ėr′ bən), *ADJECTIVE.* of or about cities or towns: *Many urban areas are crowded with people, traffic, and buildings.*

a in hat	ō in open	sh in she
ā in age	ȯ in all	th in thin
â in care	ô in order	ŦH in then
ä in far	oi in oil	zh in measure
e in let	ou in out	ə =a in about
ē in equal	u in cup	ə =e in taken
ėr in term	ů in put	ə =i in pencil
i in it	ü in rule	ə =o in lemon
ī in ice	ch in child	ə =u in circus
o in hot	ng in long	

Acknowledgments

Text

78–81 "The Ray" and "The Anglerfish" from *In The Swim: Poems And Paintings* by Douglas Florian, copyright © 1997 by Douglas Florian, used by permission of Harcourt, Inc.

Illustrations

2, 6, 18–25 Liz Callen; **32, 44–51, 139** Jane McCreary; **40** Susan J. Carlson; **58, 70–77** John Sandford; **107** Meredith Johnson; **110, 124–131** Joy Allen; **132** R. J. Shay

Photographs

Every effort has been made to secure permission and provide appropriate credit for photographic material. The publisher deeply regrets any omission and pledges to correct errors called to its attention in subsequent editions.

Unless otherwise acknowledged, all photographs are the property of Scott Foresman, a division of Pearson Education.

Photo locators denoted as follows: Top (T), Center (C), Bottom (B), Left (L), Right (R), Background (Bkgd).

Opener: (CL) ©Will & Deni McIntyre/Getty Images, (L) ©Elizabeth Kreutz/NewSport/Corbis, (CR) ©Stephen Bond/Alamy Images, (CR) ©Bettmann/Corbis, (BC) ©Tyler Stableford/Getty Images; **1** ©Elizabeth Kreutz/NewSport/Corbis; **2** ©Zigy Kaluzny/Getty Images; **3** (T) ©Stephen Bond/Alamy Images, (CR) ©Christian Kober/Alamy Images, (BR) ©Jana Leon/Getty Images; **5** ©Stockbyte Platinum/Getty Images; **6** (TR) ©Andre Jenny/Alamy Images, (CR, R) Getty Images, (BR) ©Stacy D. Gold/Getty Images; **7** ©Roy Morsch/Zefa/Corbis; **8** ©Adrian Wilson/Getty Images; **9** (BL) ©Simon Watson/Botanica/Jupiter Images, (CL) ©Andre Jenny/Alamy Images, (TL) Comstock Images, (BCL) ©Juan Houston/Getty Images; **10** (CL) Prints & Photographs Division [LC-USZ62-19448]/Library of Congress, (BL) ©Dennis MacDonald/Alamy Images; **11** Getty Images; **12** ©David Kennedy/Show Me Photos; **13** ©Brucemore Collection; **14** (T) Illinois Historic Preservation Agency, (CL) Getty Images; **15** ©John Crouch; **16** ©Courtesy of Old School Square Cultural Arts Center; **17** (T, CR) ©Wolfgang Kaehler/Corbis; **26** (CR, C) Getty Images, (BR) ©Garry Black/Masterfile Corporation; **27** (TL) Getty Images, (BL) ©Richard Nowitz/Getty Images, (CL) ©Stacy D. Gold/Getty Images; **28** Getty Images; **29** (CL, BR) Getty Images; **30** ©Roy Morsch/Zefa/Corbis; **31** Getty Images; **32** (TR) ©Bob Collier Photos/Sygma/Corbis, (CR) ©Tim Tadder/NewSport/Corbis, (BR) ©Bettmann/Corbis; **33** ©Zigy Kaluzny/Getty Images; **34** (BR) ©James King-Holmes/Photo Researchers, Inc., (BR) ©Bob Collier Photos/Sygma/Corbis, (T) Getty Images; **35** (B) Getty Images, (T) ©Chase Jarvis/Getty Images, (BR) ©Bob Collier Photos/Sygma/Corbis, (BL) ©Ed Kashi/Corbis; **36** (Bkgd) ©Tim Tadder/NewSport/Corbis, (C) Getty Images; **37** Getty Images; **38** ©Elizabeth Kreutz/NewSport/Corbis; **39** AP Images; **40** Getty Images; **41** ©Matt Turner/Allsport/Getty Images; **42** (Bkgd) Getty Images, (T) AP Images; **43** ©Carlo Allegri/Getty Images; **52** (TR) ©Bettmann/Corbis, (BL) Corbis; **53** (BL) ©Bettmann/Corbis, (TR) Alan Williams/©DK Images; **54** (BR, TL) ©Bettmann/Corbis; **55** (TR) ©Beethoven House Bonn/Dagli Orti/The Art Archive, (CL) ©Culver Pictures, Inc./SuperStock; **56** ©Zigy Kaluzny/Getty Images; **57** ©Stephen Bond/Alamy Images; **58** (CR) ©George Lep/Getty Images, (TR) ©Andrew Darrington/Alamy Images; **59** ©Joe McDonald/Corbis; **60** (T) ©Lynn Stone/Animals Animals/Earth Scenes, (C) ©Norbert Rosing/Getty Images, (BR) ©Paul Nicklen/Getty Images; **61** (BR) ©Andrew Darrington/Alamy Images, (TR) ©Steve Knott/Alamy Images; **62** ©Eastcott Momatiuk/Getty Images; **64** (CL) ©Joel Sartore/Getty Images, (B) ©Clive Druett/Papilio/Corbis; **65** ©Dr. Billy Higginbotham/Texas Cooperative Extension; **66** AP Images; **67** ©Steven Buglass/Alamy Images; **68** ©Bob Daemmrich/Corbis; **69** ©George Lep/Getty Images; **82** ©Joe McDonald/Corbis; **83** (Bkgd) ©Canopy Photography/Veer, Inc., (TL) Getty Images; **84** (BR, TC) Getty Images, (CR) Jupiter Images, (TCR) ©Bryan & Cherry Alexander Photography/Alamy Images, (TR) ©Will & Deni McIntyre/Getty Images; **85** (BR) Getty Images, (L) ©Stephen Mallon/Getty Images; **86** (T) Getty Images, (CR) ©Yang Liu/Corbis, (TL) ©Carlos Navajas/Getty Images, (B) ©Will & Deni McIntyre/Getty Images; **87** (B) Getty Images, (C) ©Andre Jenny/Alamy Images; **88** (TL) ©Yellow Dog Productions/Getty Images, (TR) ©Mark Segal/Getty Images, (BR) Getty Images; **89** (B) Getty Images, (BR) ©Tore Kjeilen/LexicOrient, (T) ©Stan Armington/Lonely Planet Images; **90** (C) ©Jake Rajs/Getty Images, (B) ©Rex Butcher/Getty Images; **91** (TR) Getty Images, (L) ©Stock Connection/Alamy Images; **92** (T) ©Christian Kober/Alamy Images, (CL) Hemera Technologies; **93** (TR) Getty Images, (B) ©Roy Rainford/Getty Images; **94** (TC) Getty Images, (B) ©Neil McAllister/Alamy Images, (TR) Hemera Technologies; **95** (CL) ©Kyko Haga/HAGA/The Image Works, Inc., (T) ©Michael Freeman/Corbis; **96** (TC) Getty Images, (B) ©Bryan & Cherry Alexander Photography/Alamy Images; **97** (BR) Hemera Technologies, (T, TL) ©Peter Arnold, Inc./Alamy Images; **98** (BC) ©David Frazier/PhotoEdit, (Bkgd) Getty Images; **99** The Granger Collection, NY; **100** (Bkgd) Getty Images, (BR) Hemera Technologies, (C) The Granger Collection, NY; **101** (TR) Jupiter Images, (C) ©Bettmann/Corbis; **102** (Bkgd) Getty Images, (B) Jupiter Images; **103** Jupiter Images; **104** (Bkgd, BL) Getty Images, (TC) Hemera Technologies, (BR) ©Bill Aron/PhotoEdit; **105** Hemera Technologies, (B) ©Gabe Palmer/Corbis; **106** (BR) ©Shalom Ormsby/Getty Images, (BC, TR, CL, C, CR) Getty Images, (BL) ©Tyler Stableford/Getty Images; **107** Hemera Technologies; **108** (TR) Getty Images, (R) ©Stephen Mallon/Getty Images; **109** ©White Cross Productions/Getty Images; **110** (CR) Getty Images, (BR, TR) Hemera Technologies; **111** ©Tom & Dee Ann McCarthy/Corbis; **113** (TCL, BL) Hemera Technologies; **115** ©Royalty-Free/Corbis; **116** (B) ©David Katzenstein/Corbis, (Bkgd) Getty Images; **117** (T) ©Orlando/Three Lions/Getty Images, (B) Getty Images, (TL) ©John Florea/Getty Images; **118** (Bkgd, B) Getty Images, (TL) ©John Florea/Getty Images; **119** ©Columbia/Sony/Chan Kam Chuen/The Kobal Collection; **120** Getty Images; **121** (T) ©Andrew Kolb/Masterfile Corporation, (B) ©Royalty-Free/Corbis; **122** (Bkgd, B) Getty Images, (TL) ©Tony Freeman/PhotoEdit; **123** ©Jana Leon/Getty Images; **132** (TR, BL) Hemera Technologies; **133** Hemera Technologies; **134** ©Tom & Dee Ann McCarthy/Corbis; **135** ©Paul Nicklen/Getty Images; **136** (TR) ©Bob Daemmrich/Corbis, (BR) ©Andrew Darrington/Alamy Images; **137** ©Joel Sartore/Getty Images; **138** AP Images; **140** (TR) ©Zigy Kaluzny/Getty Images, (BR) ©Jana Leon/Getty Images; **141** ©Tore Kjeilen/LexicOrient; **142** ©Wolfgang Kaehler/Corbis; **143** ©Jake Rajs/Getty Images